DISTANT KINSHIPS

poems of

ANTHONY BERNINI

A.P.D.

The alternative press for Albany's Poets

2002

The Barbara Holland Series #3

Library of Congress Cataloging-in-Publication Data

Bernini, Anthony
  Distant Kinships

  Control Number: 2001099965
  ISBN 0-9714631-2-3

FIRST EDITION

This book was set in Bauer Bodoni.

Text/Cover designed by Nicholas A. Bernini

Cover photo: Elm and Rock, Central Park, New York City, by Paul Peterson

A.P.D.
c/o Wilcox
280 South Main Ave.
Albany, NY 12208

to Isabella, Domenica, Massimilliano,
and Joseph,
who gave me my parents.

Table of Contents

❦

Table of Contents *(Continued)*

Introduction

We Have Not Traveled Far

For the poet, a poem is a way to be one's true self. For the reader, a poem is a way to understand and feel one's true self. Without teaching, a poet helps us to learn who we truly are. Great poetry has the purity of first sight.

Beginning with the Romantic poets, the imagination of the individual, and not the collective memory of the group, has been considered the source of poetic power. For many modern poets, the art is a way of gaining access to the unconscious of an individual or the collective unconscious of a group. But however one looks at it, poetry is a manner of using language that is different from ordinary speech and all forms of prose writing.

An anonymous poet gave marvelous advice to any writer, "Don't learn the tricks of the trade. Learn the trade." Since 1963, I have had the pleasure of watching Anthony Bernini grow as a person and learn the trade of a poet. During the fall of 1964 and spring of 1965, his poems arrived on small pieces of yellow note pad paper. Invariably, the poems were accompanied by long, detailed, discursive letters—Salingerian in style—that elaborated on the events of daily life that later found poetic expression.

At the time, Anthony and I, along with our friends and fellow students, were experiencing for the first time the poetic visions of the ages. The names are still magic: Chaucer, Marlowe, Shakespeare, Marvell, Blake, Wordsworth, Coleridge, Donne, Keats, Shelley, Byron, Dante, Beaudelaire, Rimbaud, Rilke, Poe, Whitman, Dickinson, Melville, Gerard Manly Hopkins, A.E. Houseman, W.B. Yeats, Rupert Brooke, Wilfred Owen, T.S. Eliot, Robert Frost, Wallace Stevens, Robinson Jeffers, E.E. Cummings and Alfeo Marzi, the "Poet of the Bronx."

In 1966 and 1967, Anthony and I had the pleasure of spending a number of evenings in the home of Dr. Marzi, then a professor at Fordam University, during which all three of us shared our new poems with one another. It was a thrill for two young writers to be the guest of a published poet and to be taken seriously as practitioners of the art and craft of poetry.

But the poet that most influenced the young Bernini was Bob Dylan. One wonderful summer afternoon, around the time of the release of *Highway 61 Revisited*, I met Anthony in Columbus Circle in Manhattan. We found a suitable patch of concrete and sat down on the sidewalk, ignored by the passersby preoccupied with their busy-ness. (It was at that moment I noticed that Bernini's hairstyle was coming to resemble

Dylan's.) He handed me another collection of yellow note pad papers. On the first page was a poem that has stayed with me for nearly 40 years, titled *Observation No. 4* (Dylanesque title, no?). With this one poem, I became a devoted reader of Bernini and have read him avidly ever since.

The refrain of this marvelous poem has, unfortunately, been proven true over the ensuing decades, "We have not traveled far." Wherever one casts one's glance, it is apparent that despite its technological achievements, the human animal has not advanced significantly as a species. The great books of the great civilizations are testaments to this.

As young poets struggle to find their own voices, the influence of their poetic mentors is often clearly evident in their work. In Bernini's adolescence, the imprint of Dylan and Cummings was apparent in much of his work, as was the voice of Eliot. But as he matured as a person and developed as a writer, Bernini's own voice emerged and his own style developed, a style that could be described, in a purely non-academic way, as "romantic classicism." After reading this volume, decide for yourself if it is an appropriate description.

Dickinson and Melville wrote in obscurity, Joyce in exile; Robinson Jeffers in self-imposed "exile" in the untrammeled wilderness of the California coast; Wallace Stevens while serving time in the insurance industry. Bernini labors as an attorney in Albany, NY and lives and writes near Troy, NY. His work is now known to a small but widening audience. This book is the first collection of his poetry to be published. It is my hope that many more will follow.

In *Distant Kinships* we meet the inhabitants of Bernini's world. They are us and the people we know: Mac, the fisherman; Sally who has just lost her most cherished tree; the matriarch of the family; the former owner of Bernini's present home; the local butcher; the woman who is losing her home to a dam, and the children who are our hope.

With him, we go to the places we all go: to church, the donut store, the library, the beach, the farm, the park, the funeral, Cayuga Lake, Mesopotamia, Manhattan and then down to the river. We meet our fellow animals—an owl, a bear, an unseen creature in the dark, fireflies, sparrows—and learn the lessons they have to teach. We travel to Venice, Mendocino, and Providence, Rhode Island. We celebrate spring, autumn, summer and winter. We mourn the loss of family, friends and neighbors.

In Bernini's poetry, we encounter love and the loss of love; generosity of spirit and cruelty; mystery and understanding; the profound in the mundane; the hope of the pessimistic optimist. And there is humor in his work; a wry, realistic yet tender smile for a confused humanity that doesn't seem to have much of a chance but carries on anyway, not having much of a choice.

In the title poem, *Distant Kinships*, Bernini writes,

> *"Without a sound old starlight slips*
> *an arm around the duskblind world*
> *where death reveals distant kinships."*

Death may reveal distant kinships to us, but Bernini's poetry shows us the intimate connections we all have to one another, to the other life forms on earth, to ourselves, and to Life itself. Some or all of these connections may be severed, temporarily or perhaps permanently, but these poems restore that connection, at least while one is reading—so keep reading!

We humans may not have traveled far as a species but Anthony Bernini has traveled far, as a man and as a poet. And you, Dear Reader, now have the pleasure of walking with him for part of that journey.

Michael Mannion
Langton Matravers, Dorset, England
May 2001

Acknowledgements

Waiting Near Murvale has previously appeared in the eleventh MUSE, *On The High Line* has previously appeared in The Orphic Lute; *Someone Is Laughing* has previously appeared in Open Mike: The Albany Anthology.

Michael Mannion is the author of two novels, *Death Cloud* and *Colleen*, and such nonfiction works as *Project Mindshift: The Re-Education of the American Public Concerning Extraterrestrial Life*, and *Frankenstein Foods: What Genetically Modified Foods Mean to You and Your Family*. He is the Author of two forthcoming books, *The New American Medicine* and *Erin's Daughters*, a novel.

The poems selected for this volume reflect the astute editorial suggestions of Mary Ann Cleaves.

The Owl Who Stole A Photographer's Eye

The barred owl in a magazine,
her captured corona of quill
mantled around hard golden eyes
was never seen,
a creature intended to fill
the racks that hang in waiting rooms
or lie flat on dead wood
with jam and cream.

Who in those rooms could hear
the thread's incessant spin,
the silent sweep begin,
raptor and wind harmonize
before a talon closed
around the prying eyes.
The barred owl framed in a snap
hangs in the air like tick and chime
when clocks map teeming space,
the shadow of an unseen hand
that glides over the numbered face.

Waiting Near Murvale

When the Trayner place was sold
with its henhouse and an inground pool
no one mentioned them. Yet they were there
like bramble in the background, out of focus:
a cultivator and the horsedrawn plow.
We found them lean with rust, at rest
along the wire fence that sets
the field off from itself.

Within the waiting wheels, the ready steel,
the springs stiff with impatience,
corn is standing deeper than graves are dug,
and lettuce thick as water in a well.
Still, not enough to give hands to the handles.

What can we do with plows and shares but paint them black,
plant them in the garden for the children.
We go indoors to do our chores.
Beyond the treeline small birds fly through heavy rain.

Before The Butcher Fell From Grace

When my child's nose knew how to think
the butcher shop filled me with flesh-
scented sawdust spilling in my small
swamped shoes and tempting me to sink.
I felt the cool dense air enfold
my unresisting face, draw me
to the white enamel case
to commune with the peaceful dead.
I could feel the raggety rip
of thick brown wrapping paper pulled
from an enormous roll and held
against a black wrought iron strip,
preposterously heavy.
The butcher's hands were rich landscapes
scored with swollen veins, majestic
knuckled ridges, muscled brown swales
peopled by thickwaisted fingers.
In those days I felt no need to charge
his hands as psychological
suspects, so ominously large,
so capable of homicide,
trafficking in cholesterol.
He reassured me that my mom could slide
her slippers safely down beside
his bed at any hour.

The Providence Atheneum

The Providence Atheneum
sits still like other libraries
almost obscured by the surrounding blur,
as if in the midst of asteroids.

The intensity of dark wood, of leather,
the marble busts, always of generals,
cannot diminish the prevailing
absense of things, the concavity
of visions in suspense.

Through the rain come little children
trailing parents and wet shoes
to watch movies in the morning
while words from distant reaches wait
in books loaded like honeycombs
to quicken dreams.

Before The Storm

Before thunder silences the land,
before the deluge is discharged,
the forces brought to bear upon
the earth converge, like mist and sand
that gather to themselves until
the rivers swell and mountains rise.

Before thunder guns across the land,
before their reason has been purged,
they gather in a vast footprint
that crashed among them long ago
to count the length and breadth of fear
and spill their love out on the stones.

Before madness seizes every hand,
before the battlements are forged,
the ancient memories are spent.
The young among them cannot know
how deafening the voice of fear,
how lost the many have become.

Before thunder silences the land,
before the frenzy and the smoke,
war seems as natural as a storm.

The Chosen Ones

Children have been chosen
for public disregard,
touched by a laying on of hands grown hard,
children for public sacrifice,
beasts in a lean season.
Yet there will be no bloody invocation.
No one will lead the victims forth
from exhalted isolation.
They will take shelter in each other
beneath the unattended altars,
back of all the broken fences.

The chosen ones are hard to count,
blinking in cut fields
like rabbits in the hunt
seen from a hilltop cowled in winter sky,
countless as the blown down apples
in orchards gone to ruin,
or through the dark city meadows,
flashing like mica chips that catch the light
and vanish at the sidewalk underfoot
in the brickthrown shadows.

In towns sunk in the tired hills
the grip of empire can palm
only sand from each old road's thin shoulders
where stray dogs and defiant daffodils
share an irresolute eternal rule.

Remembrance Of Mac

When Mac stood up in his green boat to jig,
the lake in sway at the tip of his rod,
the shores receded and the sky grew big,
and deep below there stirred a demigod.

The invocation of his dancing hand
was more than mortal men could understand.
But through the gate of clouds others were drawn
to watch the egg of night break into dawn.

He stood between two worlds, a living mark.
The line ran through his hand from dark to dark.
Like touch unseen, as strong as faith it lie,
that water's heart could beat up to the sky.

Stone Church

Your eyes cannot roam without meeting one
riding a hill or filling a hollow,
permanence massed greyly
defying the seasons,
always with that finger pointed skyward
as if the heavens must be more
or we less than we are.

What do I really see, a mile away?
How much scraping of the earth, how many
loveless bones consigned to ash
are melded in those walls?
When those doors are thrown open
and intolerence itself issues forth
to gather in the world like sheep,
what remains at the bottom of that box
if not imperishable hope?
What do I really see, besides
the swallows in the folds of stone.

Farm For Sale

A roadside sign says Farm For Sale,
no more. There must be some mistake.
They cannot sell the sunlight in the vale
like produce in a crate.

What visitation grips the folks,
what did they see that prowls the fields,
what swollen-bellied thing that stalks
and lays to waste all that life yields?

The farmer must he sell the Spring,
the morning moist and glistening?
And where he goes will life be kind?
And can that thing be far behind?

Who You Were

You rested weathered on a wooden chair
in folds of old flannel as if fallen
from a clothesline billowed with color,
missing and presumed lost.
The colors that covered you had faded,
I had to look through bare fabric to see you.
Who you were has willed this world to me,
this mystery of mountains, these cleft cliffs.
They know the stream of you, swollen by Spring,
filling the defile that waits for me.

Orestes for long years lay unattended,
his peloponnese landscape languishing,
diminished by a plunder of neglect.
Bones in a box by the time they found him.
I need not wait for oracles,
for eagles who circle your grave.
So as you rest I must persist,
shaken from sleep, summoned to save
who you were.

Death Watch

There in the bed
within the tubes and tape
you settle like old beams
toward the ground.
What can be as wide
as the windowful of world
in your flickering eye
while you gather in
particles of rage
to hurl at the ferment of flowers?

Finally your hand
stops reaching in the air.
Others must decide
what stays, what goes with you.
You smile with relief.
They wait near the door
like bags of grief
you will not have to open.
The room shakes
like December's final leaf.

The Matriarch's Funeral Dress

That blue appears nowhere in nature,
not in Bay Ridge, where the sandstone
always can absorb a little rain.

The dress was bunched like packing paper
as if what was fragile should survive
the disembodied strength of her.
That blue which cannot rest in place,
that bridesmaids are committed to,
was heaped on her, blue frosting over bread.

I knew her when she wielded power
absolutely, with a wooden spoon,
forgiving all, nothing forgotten.

Then, her dark vitality was cloaked
in undertones mottled with plum and basil,
all before her stirred until it settled.

Her strength scattered and brought me here
hemmed in by crosses and freak orchids,
my memories concealed in mourning clothes.

Mass Of The Resurrection

There is no empty space like the morning
after death steals the night without warning.
In the boundless street dispossessed by sun
we wait to greet the dead. Time is undone.

Her sons are staggered, sit concussed by bells,
borne deeper into occult rituals.
In a distant pew with a seemly grief
we speak of memories, need no belief.

In swells of smoke, receding bells,
some unremitting intrigue dwells.
They rise and leave, restored to sight
within a column of hard light.

Forward steps her sister on the cold stone,
her eyes flung wide as that lost field
where, braced by flowers, wild they reeled,
fierce with beauty, fearlessly alone.

Carpe Diem

I fear to love you in this fragile land,
this turbulence conjoined by frogs, by spiderwebs.
You would reassure me. Where you stand
your words fall around me in multitudes
like pods from a tree, narrow and thin,
filled with the certainty of numbers.
You smile like trees sway, imperceptably,
deep in the trunk. I look away.

The pods twirl thousands down to the tight earth
until one pointed tip penetrates and stands.
It will be some time before the blind seed
sends fingers through the packed detritus, finds
what is waiting and fertile, time enough
for grip to fail, desert the hand.
So I am grateful now you ravished me
some time before the trembling strands won't hold
the rending earth, the waiting sea.

Bear Fact

One day a black bear came to Troy
and climbed into an old oak tree.

He passed unrecognized through towns
past chickens and the sleeping hounds
down from the dark exhalted grounds,
the mountain gleaming porphyry.

Over each fence and ivied wall
the black bear had the wherewithall
to pass unnoticed as a flea
and climb into an old oak tree.

Soon people stirred, they gathered round,
they scratched their heads and pawed the ground
and puzzled at what unrenowned
determined perspicacity
united bear and old oak tree.

A Voice In The Night

Beyond the lawn, the dark of trees
breaks an extremity of voice
flinted at the tip of shafted breath,
roughhewn from pressing need piercing
night's intricately sightless shape.
I may never know a bobcat
from a lonely gonewild mouser
but buried in an unmarked place
where this voice strikes the deafdead part of me
my ancestors could sift a voice in flight,
pluck out its lust or desperate prayer
or know the danger that it held at bay.
The animal unsettles me
to know more than this wistful curiosity,
enough to disinter my origins,
restore the listener to light.

Before Spring

Before Spring comes everything
rushing through brief interminable days
into relentless evening,
hurtling through the sharp air
too fast to cast shadows,
black things in pale light
like so many sparrows.

Where do they go, all the sparrows?
There can be only so many
Warm spaces, so many
dry places in the black
branches of the clenched earth.
Do they stream through thick night
to huddle at the roof of the world,
like boxes of everything massed in the attic
always out of season?

Wherever they are sunlight is
moving slow in their dreams
while they uncurl their feet
and sing without reason.

Real Estate

Before the house is closed may I come in,
that I might recollect what may have been:
the fire speaking softly while we glow
the Christmas lights seen through the blinding snow.

Before you pull the curtains from the pane,
before the floor is cold and bare again,
the fern can drape itself around the sill,
the cat can curl its tail against the chill.

Like blossoms waiting in the frozen ground
a home waits in this building that you found.
As surely as we dance before we creep
our birthright is to dream before we sleep.

Until We Meet Again

I will find you in a room with white walls
under high plaster medallions
dense with wild grape and long oak leaves.
I will hear your sighs rise to the clusters,
be folded in before they fade.

A room set within a Tuscan villa,
held by brick in common bond and dark woods,
granite stone crowning windows wide.
Long after the sun breeches the tower
early light will linger round your bare arms.

I can walk from impoverished shop malls
past the silenced cars on heatbuckled roads.
There is room beneath the tall eaves
where spearmint grows and jonnyjumpups flower
to stand enchanted in the shade.

Revolt

He favors cacti,
keeps them in dark soil
in pottery confinements on Italian tile.

What do they know, astonished Cereus,
Echinopsis cinctured in that sweet earth,
Opuntia immersed in such rich blackness.

They know the vain reach of lost limbs
sweeping through dry immensities
waiting for one drop from the desert's crinkled eye.

Now their fingers spike
through winter's white air in his deserted house,
reach for nothing, hold their succulence within.

Far from home he thinks they will be waiting
after long neglect
for his spoonful of dirt.

Thoughtless, the cacti torch
through the surrounding chill
with crimson bloom.

A Gift From Venice

This candy cast in glass
you carried out of Venice
in a paper bag, is it descended
from the white comely bull,
a godchild born to broken flight
formed in the uncertain final hours
of a dream's brief season,
last of its kind?
Did it throw a silken lasso
loose around your bewildered neck,
choose you for your strong silent wings
to bring it to the light at my window
that it might like its father soon transmute
into a new redoubt of form?

In early light when heavenly
bodies are wont to slide away
its red helix wavers.
A great snake rises in the mist.

At Flagstones

Where the Esopus scores the banks
deep beneath the wavering birch
an eagle shot over the stream
immense within the sheltered crease
with folded wings distending space,
propelled through history.
Those talons dropped a line of kings
into the sure arms of a boy
before descending to the stream
to lift a rainbow for its catch.
The vision was that fleet.
Continuing along, the stream
among the flagstones gathered song
where rock and water meet.
Returning to its lofty perch
the bird leaves some iconic trace
wherever, making fragile peace,
meet mankind and nobility.

Moment at Mendocino

On its bouldered impermanence of cliff
tenacious Mendocino courts the sea
while clinging to a border set adrift
by seafoam fingers white with work.

Sheltered between monoliths and redwoods
Mendocino cultures dissolution.
All the old paint fades to seasky blue.

Back from shifting cliffs stands one old cabin.
A seer, angular, soft, dark, seeing,
offers us slow wine from Mariposa,
her proteus brings abalone shells.
We talk of what to wish for come the dawn.

We walk. The dirt road blooms a smiling boy.
From pale vivid hands he gives us cookies
heavy with slowmelting seconds.

A moment carved out of a redwood trunk
is fixed atop the empty Mason Hall,
a graven longrobed Time standing behind
a seated maiden whose cinnamon braid
is dangling through the ageless working hands.
Here where cookies hold together
while the riptide topples shores
no one knows if the braid is drawn tighter
or loosening to meet the ocean wind.

On The High Line

First these mountains came, then Tintic the Ute,
both from imperishable origins.
They crystallized, became the Tintic Range,
stratum of dream in which dreamers took root.
Priest-conquerors beheld them and shrank back,
pronounced their beauty unredeemable.

Then came small hard men with sharp eyes
raking the green swells for ore float,
outcroppings of fable and dream.
Steel drills, muscles, hammers chanted.
Far off, dark suits, pale men heard them.
Overshadowing the sage
timbered iron blossoms bloomed,
ingersols and stopers penetrated,
money married men to stone.

Now the headframes stand bereft over the hollows.
One old hard rock miner drives the high line
holding safe these punctured hills, his lovers.
Mule deer weaving through the sage like dolphin
where Silver City lies, transformed to dream,
bestir the sweet sage blown against the vibrant sky.
Reports of Tintic's death are premature.

Galena

You would have given me sagacity,
all the valor and compassion
that flesh an uncle's open hand.
Because you mined your virtues from the earth
you gave a sample of galena ore,
native lead, dull grey and very heavy.
To show what might be locked inside
you chiseled one end off-
a silvery window streaming at me
glittering like a skinned knee
with unspoken trial.

Airport x-rays scanning my galena
found a Black Hole in my baggage,
repelling pretense of disclosure.
They took us off. I smiled inscrutably.
I kept my flight with verity,
perseverence, valor-
the third part of the vein,
what remains behind in the furnace.

The Cedar Boat

Before the Mississippi starts its run
Down through the continent from Big Gull Lake
its waters pass a fir tree facing West,
trunk limblessly defiant,
fast against voracious wind.
Beside this tree was placed the cedar boat.
Tilted finally on the blunted rock,
now upside down it holds the land
like spent seabirds might stand, with hanging wings.

The unbroken cedar has the color
of wind enfolded in the water's creases.
It is the grey of ageless churning,
of lake and sky displaced to chaos.
The cedar, though unbroken, has been thinned.
The breath of the lake is upon it now
to claim its own. The wind's voice is the wind
I hear among gravestones worn like old teeth.

Below The Conklingville Dam

I

A woman of great age stood in the fields
around the Sacandaga, where the floods
were to be loosed over the land for gain.
Her age draws back the elements again,
earth, air, fire, water, the fundaments.
The faithful shores, blue waters and green earth,
the sky descending on dyhedral wings,
the farflung fires, coalesce again
into a precreation pinwheeling
where still she forms her untold history.

You can see those elements infusing
in any great endurer, like that whale,
mountainously white, churning the borders
of familiar densities, encrusted
with barnacles and ropes and flaming eyes.

They had come to evict her, uniforms,
badges, guns and papers, tools of schemers.
The land had been condemned. But there she stood.

Her apprehensive eyes were pale and full,
storm skies thickening to lower deluge.
She apprehended them the way a tree
must know the air loaded with crackling tongues
around each twig, before the storm begins.

(continued)

II

She lived above a deep preglacial gorge
that whispered with the valley's smallest voice.
A century before, the forest floor
as deep as the sky kept all things that die.
Then one day came the bandsaw's glittering teeth.
First went the great white pines, but not enough,
the tanbark flayed, the hardwoods carried off.
Diminishment can never get enough.
The cannibal is crushing his own bones.
She watched them grind through 1929,
denude the valley to an open grave.
By year's end, every barn broken and burned.
Now sound was stilled, became sluiced granite core,
rock cover and earth fill. All voice was damned,
the grave marked by the Dam at Conklingville.

III

Her eyes left the contrived shores, fell like stones,
broke down through the occupying waters,
found the untended fields below.
The topsoil had bled dark the shallow lake,
deepening her sadness into anger.
Ages telescoped and tumbled through her.
She recalled swinging down sheer water walls
at the world's swamped summit, in the deluge
that swept her clinging to the earth's last peak
when all the rivers raged to scour the scrub,
rub off the scrofulous from every twig,
and all her kind except Deucalion
were washed into the inky saturate
that turned the skies into a pious grave.
She prayed the gods would let her propagate.
Purification carried off all crime
but parasites were waiting in the slime.
Now they float over the fields in party boats,
besotted on the shallow slick of greed.
Let them bloat. She will grow small, wait nearby
like the mice who trail behind the thresher
knowing there is something left to harvest.
Exploitation ticks in its short season
until one oblivion is splintered
by the hunted down flukes of another.

Pantheist Humbled By A God With Hairy Arms

There is no walking in these fields
pierced by blunted stalks tempered stiff.
A hot wind prevails, whips up blood
in what blooms, yields a fanged virtue
shooting up through children.
This place is not one world away from you.

I dream of a continuum of blue,
sapphire overgrown with lavendar,
before an ancient dawn broke into hours
that dance, stealing away with me and you.
Now the sea is carried off to moat and wall,
the craters crawl with rubblestone,
not two to rub together, cast alone.

How came I to this roadhouse that I found,
has it been open since the first marked hour
moonlight spilled across a damp earth floor?
An hour less, an hour more,
a barkeep serves another blinding round,
another round of arrogant mutations,
another century cast down
between neglected destinations.

(continued)

Behind the walled words in a tangled lot,
fatal moments fixed in twisted metal
weathered in the wind: abandoned cars,
a Gordian disjunction in chrome trim.

Laboring among spent Furies
stood a solitary fieldwright,
thick arms pumping, darkly glistening.
He cleared the hard gray ground.
They say, in the roadhouse, he plants nothing
to waylay the wind, just takes the ground down,
knowing the graves go unmarked in these parts,
knows there can never be enough flowers.

Survivors

In the hard ruts of the fields
the little squash, the pumpkins no one wanted
are still growing, slowly dying,
unnoticed like balloons in an empty room
no one bothers to remove after the party.
The orange of them glimmers through the frosted mist
looking not quite red, or gone to yellow,
while they hold the furrow juice and farmer's breath
until the final harvest.
The pumpkins taken to the market place
all end up wearing someone else's face.

In This Donut Store

In this donut store
the morning passes breezelessly
beneath blue light trapped in the ceiling.
The muffle of machinery
informs the filmy air,
suggests steel vessels, implements
turning, folding
what was known into unknown.

Here against the wall
coffee thickens, turns as cool
as the sea around exhausted limbs.
In the current at the counter
customers come in and carry off
the dark vitality in paper cups,
heat to fuel dreams
for one hour more.

Someone Is Laughing

Someone is laughing unaccountably
through the gritted teeth of our rush hour,
standing with his back and the sole of one foot
comfortably touching someone else's wall
where air comes through a vent, warm and for free.

The passing suits flee with a stolen glance,
drop condemnations like litter
where the laugher has declared himself at home
with a felicity fashioned from ice.

The laughter travels to us easily.
I wonder whether anyone can hear,
struggling to move through this long winter.
Maybe some trackless path has been revealed
by the laughter's liquid sound.
I wonder until I can almost see
the music of it moving like spilled milk
that spreads along the contours of the ground
until it's found by cats who know, and wait.

Lodged

In this hotel the bed
suspends me like stored meat,
a bundle in a web,
somebody's silkbound treat.

Somewhere above my head,
below my searching feet,
I feel the webbing sway.
Others are locked away.

This comfortable dread
feels like the wind that swings
an unattended gate
and terribly swift brings
the thought that comes too late
or something that you said.

The Banks Of The Stream

I might not know the sundered heart of Palestine
if it appeared to me along the Poestenkill.
But surely, just beneath the dead
leaves pressed rigid through the year
by each new rain
something living waits.

What do I know about Jerusalem
where miracles are made
to wait for sticks and stones?

I might not hear the broken beat of that lost heart
if it was pounding there along the stream
whose sounding has the shape of tiny
thousands of passionate voices,
yet who can say it does not wait for us
along the banks, where no death can
outlive the pomegranate tree.

Before Iraq

Before Iraq, Mesopotamia.
The Land Between The Rivers does not change.
Richer than empire, the silt of ages
blinks only for Tigris, for Euphrates.
Before Iraq the Babylonians, Assyrians,
the Mongols, Turks, Circassians, the Kurds
were watching for the pale touch of the moon
to call the rivers to the waiting fields,
watching words take shape in clay
that earth could speak and people understand.

Mesopotamia, oilmongers scramble now
to cover your deep eyes, insist you have no face.
Until they coin the latest goad to slaughter,
Bluebellied Devil, Yellow Peril, Gook,
Iraq will do: four letters, less than death.
For me, Mesopotamia, the lie is late.
In my Manhattan, USA, in grammar school,
we learned that Chevrolets, George Washington
and Marilyn Monroe all sprang from your sweet cradle.

Ground View Of A Dying Soldier

In John Ringling's garden
there lies a dying Gaul
among the succulents.

Death and horticulture
bloom eternal moments
in bronze and cellulose.

A soldier's final day,
his sword fallen away,
calm cloaks him, gathers him,
awaiting his hard palms
holding off the sweet patient ground.
His lips fall unworded
around the stranger's name.

My head must touch the earth
to see, as death attends,
that steady lies the Gaul
whose eyes will not harden.

Flares

On the fourth of July at Cayuga Lake
they set the shore alight with flares
so from on high the lake appears
like someone's magnificent birthday cake,

or maybe the scene of an accident
evolving beneath the surface all year,
ready to break, that draws them near
to reconsider or repent.

Maybe they appear, from a timeless distance,
as some shared vision taking form,
or like they dare not look ahead,
the final hour of protracted dread.

Like so many fireflies
they light up the skies
beneath the unwavering moon.

Stairway Through The Park

Aged granite steps spine the hill,
rise up or descend as they will.
Rubble rings the steps, granite light
fixed in space, moving past my sight
in an unrevealed direction.
When subjected to inspection
granite naturally dissembles.
In the halflight granite trembles.

Ancient discretions bent the stone.
Layers of footfalls invoke them.
Lovers who met, lovers alone
standing long vigils unbroken.
Below, above, all overgrown,
someplace unmarked to someplace gone,
the lost borders of Babylon
bound each to each by silent stone.

Aberration In Leaf

A red persistence of maple
standing through the cold collapse of Fall
tremors the chill air like rising heat.
Neighboring trees pale into retreat,
their leaves blown in a brittle carousel
harden to a bony huddle.

The trunk holds to the living head.
The grip of its unseasonable thriving
holds my reluctant eyes
in some dreadful surmise.
What solitary greed feeds that surviving?
I walk away, among the dead.

Appreciation For A Hot Sun

Between the rimless ocean swell
and the vaulting shell of sky
where is there space enough
for that protracted blasting face
that bores through stone and bone,
unobservably alone.

From inexplicable dawn is this deity born.
Among the lizzards and the leafy things
there is worship but no faith.
Faith fuels the desperate rememberings
in darker places where the same sun brings
a harvest of long shadows.

There is creation enough where
the shuddering sea gives forth its god,
where the sands swell with fire.
Beyond the first recumbent hills
along the chilly slopes of shade
are houses set in pockets to the wind

where creation is a spark struck
from the stone face of privation.
We become divine
only in the moment of compassion.
That we can choose our gods
is miracle enough.

Windstorm

South of this port eight hundred miles
some fury wheels into the coast,
whole skys were taken with its face,
each artifice reduced to wind, dismissed,
a thing so big they named it.

They did not have to tell me it was there.
I can feel the tendrils of its terror
reaching through the flashing birch
from somewhere south, beyond the churning river,
beyond the blunted coastal hills,
from where it tore apart the seas
and overwhelmed the barrier rocks
to stir the skin under my hair.

Let the whirlwind turn without me.
Let remain uncertain the divine.
a measure of fatality
goes into every certainty,
as when mistrustful Semele
who claimed too much of the sublime
invoked the awful presence of
her lover god's full panoply
and perished for the crime.

The Desecration

At sixteen, a herd beast
flayed by the rough side of the tongue.
He takes haunted steps over hallowed ground.

Worked into the skin,
a shard of old steel,
dark, over the heart.

It hangs at an abyss
like a car careened to breathless balance
bowing to any breeze.

He stands in a hollow of whistling heat.
Within his sealed ears
an old voice, trapped.

There is no safe
repository for such pain.
Chthonic reverberations batter him.

He stops at the tombstone of an old Jew
who fought at Anzio
and played canasta.

He grips a grease pen
like a grommet gripped
over oblivion.

The black felt tongue
licks the tomb, leaves a swastika,
darkened symbol of the sun.

In the moonthin night
his whiteknuckled grip
fills a deputy's eye.

In the voiceless air
grip answers grip,
a pistol spits.

Below the spattered stone
an old Jew folds another hand.

Heart Of The Matter

Bring me somebody's head,
an ordinary head.
Not a Pavarotti,
stuffed with refined outrage,
or some beloved head,
Mother Theresa's head,
marked for public lamentation,
or the head of Charlie Manson,
swollen with hate.
Just a head, no garnish.

I would take Medusa's head.
Who could resist such power?
But any head will do
on a platter or a block of wood
or in a burlap bag.
Even the head of no one's child
lost in Rio de Janero.
A child's head, pound for pound
could sell as many papers as the Pope's
if mounted properly.

Keep the clutter in the trunk,
your vengence, your lament.
No one remembers Judith's flaming eyes.
We are held by Holofernes' vacant stare.
Always it is the head,
some nameless, silent head
that holds us by the hair.

October Snow

Then the snow fell out of season
straight down through the collapsing sky
as if over great distances.
Snow closed massively over startled leaves
until the air began to crack
as crested trees became half trees
and along the swollen river
the blurred teeth of the chain saws gorged.

Now the valleys are unclenching.
The shattered wood will burst again
with the ancient viridescence.
And in the dreams of sassafras and oak,
the tulip reveries, the storm
is white, always in season.
The trees will no more be half trees
than dreams will be half dreams.

Distant Kinships

In one sharp breath of full leafed flight
an old elm swung
down from the hovering and stare
of routed songbirds
in a feathered flailing of the air.

Where Sally stood leg deep in dying leaves
the sudden edge of newtorn space
came like a mourner's unfamiliar face.
She grieves beside the tall relic trunk
standing headless in the lawn
like an airliner gone down,
just like losing a dog, she said.

She gave the gray husk an embrace of vine.
Next Spring a shoot of clothesline
held the trunk to home while the wood
wandered on to the brink of stone.

At the top of the limbless trunk
where the elm once forked entering the night
the silent moon pools in the cut
as every thing fades out of sight.
Without a sound old starlight slips
an arm around the duskblind world
where death reveals distant kinships.

Two Walking

Is this why we walk
in the evening, for the words,
in heather where our steps vanish
parting the spent sun strewn among shadows
in the cemetery ground?
Must I leave them in a clearing,
words I cannot reach sitting down,
shed them among stone vestiges
of the receptive dead,
walking, to gain distance
while words hang above
like dust that defines a cavity
after a structural collapse?
Is this why we walk
in the wide eyed silence of hydrangeas
where deer eat apples underneath the moon?

A Christmas Poem

We join in celebration of starlight,
go searching for our Christmas tree
and hemlock for the mantleplace
in twilight passages turning to night.

So many trees have lost their roots
propped against the siding on the road
waiting to wear ornaments bestowed
by the children of some passing stranger.

At the far field of a tree farm we walk
through the wide smile of young white spruce
to a tree standing in a thick green dusk
by the indistinct border with the dark.

The tree crowned itself with small golden cones,
waited with us in a whitefingered wind
for the old man and his measuring stick
who would praise its boughs as he brought it down.

Past the fence where day lingers last
standing on the rise of no one's land
we take a hemlock's unfolded hand
braceleted with deep blue berries.

Horses watching over steep dark shoulders
steam red and green in outdoor lights.
The dogs who cannot see bay jealously,
long for rabbits and those same old stars.

Top Of The Wheel

Pacific coast, your distances
elude me. Vision drops
exhausted to your heedless sea,
slips off into your silent sand.

Bare feet tread gently on your beach.
Stilled bodies lie awake,
cling to your curve,
let the sand sleep.

When you tremble we crack,
scatter explanation.
Your terrible yawn says nothing.

Before you heave again, pale plants
will sidle through the sandy dark,
break the surface, sing of green.

Let me feel the top car quiver
on the wheel's great hump
before we plunge through night's sweet blur.

Jensen Beach

Should you go out on Jensen Beach,
stand on its vincible white neck
astride the island barrier
facing the open unbowed sea,
should you go feel the rolling peal
shake stone to sand, throw ghosts of shell
in prostrate piles of rattling speech,
don't rent beyond today.
No one stands sure on that bare neck
where renting is the will of waves.
Rather wish for quick slender feet,
sandpiper feet that wave back at the sea,
impress the sand, then fade.

About the Author

    Anthony Bernini was born in New York City, and holds degrees from Hamilton College and Albany Law School. He lives and works near Troy, New York. *Distant Kinships* is his first volume of poetry.